Fixing Your Finances:
A Practical Guide to Managing Money and Eliminating Debt

Fixing Your Finances:
A Practical Guide to Managing Money and Eliminating Debt

Ellen Ross

Ellen Ross
2016

Copyright © 2016 by Ellen Ross

All rights reserved. This book or any portion thereof may not be reproduced or used in any manner whatsoever without the express written permission of the publisher except for the use of brief quotations in a book review or scholarly journal.

First Printing: 2016

ISBN 978-1-329-87122-9

www.AskAwayBlog.com

Dedication

To my family and friends for always supporting me.

Contents

Acknowledgements ix
Preface xi
Introduction 1
Chapter 1: Evaluating Your Situation 3
Chapter 2: Creating A Budget 7
    CUTTING EXPENSES 11
Chapter 3: Creating A Cash Spending System 13
    MINI SAVINGS FUNDS 13
    CASH SPENDING BENEFITS 13
    YOU DON'T HAVE TO CARRY THEM 14
    THEY DON'T HAVE TO BE ENVELOPES 15
    USING A CARD INSTEAD OF CASH 17
    PAYING BILLS 17
    EXTRA CASH 17
    BORROWING 18
    COINS 18
Chapter 4: EMERGENCY SAVINGS 19
    USING YOUR EMERGENCY SAVINGS 20
Chapter 5: Paying Off Your Debt 21
    DEBT FREE 24
Chapter 6 – Building A Savings Fund 27
    IMPORTANCE OF A SAVINGS FUND 27
    HOW MUCH TO SAVE 27
    HOW TO SAVE 28
Chapter 7: Living Within Your Means 29
    GROCERIES 30
    MEAL PLANNING 31
Chapter 8: Credit Cards 33
    PAYING THEM OFF 33

- CREDIT SCORES 33
- STRUGGLING TO PAY YOUR DEBTS 34
- CASH TALKS 34
- CREDIT CARD REWARDS 35
- REWARDS FOR OPENING A CREDIT CARD 35
- SPECIAL FINANCING 36
- BUYING A VEHICLE 37

Chapter 9: Changes 43
- DON'T BECOME TOO SET IN YOUR WAYS 43
- LIFE HAPPENS 43
- HOLIDAYS 43

Chapter 10: Lifestyle Changes 45
- ADDITIONAL EMPLOYMENT 45
- HOW YOU SPEND YOUR FREE TIME 45
- MAKE EXTRA CASH WHENEVER YOU CAN 45
- GETTING ORGANIZED 46
- GOODS vs. EXPERIENCES 46

Chapter 11: My Story 47

Chapter 12: How I Live Now 51

Chapter 13: Just the Beginning 53

Appendices 55
- ADDITIONAL RESOURCES 61

Acknowledgements

I would like to thank my family, friends, and everyone who has read my blog and supported my writing over the years. Without your positive motivation and constructive criticism along the way, this book would not have been possible.

Preface

As a blogger, I've posted numerous articles about budgeting, debt, healthy spending habits, and saving money. I wrote this book as a way to get all of that advice in one central place for others to use as a guide to get themselves in better financial shape. I am by no means an expert in the financial field, but the advice in this book is what worked for me to become debt free and stop living paycheck to paycheck.

Getting your finances in order isn't just about making up a budget; it's about knowing where your money goes, spending it wisely, and building up a healthy savings fund. Even if you've already mastered one of these aspects, I'm sure you'll still find this book beneficial.

Please remember that this book is meant to be read from start to finish. You can follow along and work on some of the initial steps as you go, but please read this book in its entirety at least once so that you know what aspects of fixing your finances lie ahead. Later, you can refer back to certain chapters to help you make adjustments to your budget or debt pay down plan.

So sit down and begin the rewarding process of fixing your finances so that you can take back control of your money and never let it stress you out again!

Ellen Ross

Introduction

For as long as I can remember, money had always been a source of stress in my life. I constantly had a ridiculous amount of credit card debt, a zero balance in my savings account, and within 2 days of receiving my paycheck I would be eagerly awaiting the next one. I knew that eventually I would need to get my finances in order, but I had no idea where or how to start.

I had a normal life growing up, with both parents working full time and the occasional financial difficulties that most families experience. When I started my first job at the age of 16, I didn't understand the concept of managing money. I opened my first checking account and received my first line of credit in the form of a credit card. I would use it for things like getting my car to pass inspection, which usually cost me hundreds of dollars each time. What I failed to realize was that if I didn't pay my credit card balance down promptly, it would spiral out of control; and that's just what it did.

By the age of 22, I had over $20,000 in credit card debt and I was spending money just to feel good inside. I would go shopping when I felt stressed or bored and buy whatever caught my eye. My habits were very unhealthy but it wasn't until I hit rock bottom a few years later that I realized I needed to make some major changes or I would never get out of debt.

Rock bottom for me was when I could no longer afford my lifestyle even after I reduced every expense possible. The only solution was for me to move back home. While not everyone has that option, there are other steps you can take to turn your situation around.

I never understood why I lived paycheck to paycheck for so long, but when I did my research, took advice from experts, and focused my energy on fixing my finances, it turned my life around. I'm now almost 30 years old with no credit card debt, a house of my own, and a decent savings fund. I can account for every single dollar I have and where it goes. I have excellent spending habits and consider myself very disciplined with money. Many people have asked me how I did it and what they should do to follow in my footsteps; so here I am – presenting all of my advice to you in this book. You don't have to follow it exactly how it's laid out, but if you use it as a guide and adjust it to fit your lifestyle, the payoff will be fantastic.

Chapter 1: Evaluating Your Situation

Most people are overwhelmed at the thought of their finances, but you can't be expected to manage your money if you don't know where you stand. Many of us have no clue where our money goes each month since we neglect to account for every single purchase. This first chapter is going to help you take a long hard look at your finances and determine your current situation. I'll show you how to figure out exactly how much you make, how much your monthly obligations are, and how you've been spending your money.

Step 1: Categorize & Evaluate Expenses

Start by gathering the last 12 months' worth of bank statements and receipts. You will use this documentation to see where your money has been going. If you use a debit or credit card for most purchases, those expenses should be reflected on bank statements. If you're a cash spender, then hopefully you've been saving your receipts.

Next, you should gather some highlighters, markers, or colored pencils. You will use these to circle or highlight expenses one by one and assign each one to a category.

Your expenses will likely fall under the following categories:

Bills - Bills include mortgage, rent, car payments, cell phone, utilities, insurance, and credit card minimum payments.

Medical Expenses - Medical expenses include copays for prescriptions and doctor's appointments.

Living Expenses - Living expenses are things that you and your family need to survive such as groceries, clothing, toiletries, vehicle expenses, and pet supplies.

Bi-Monthly/Quarterly Expenses - Some expenses are paid on a monthly basis while others are paid quarterly. You will want to divide the yearly cost by 12 to determine the cost per month.

Fun Expenses - Fun expenses include dining out, monthly subscriptions, movie tickets, and anything else you spend money on for enjoyment.

Other - Some expenses won't have a category. These could be impulse buys like the jeans you picked up at Target when you originally went in for groceries. While clothing is a necessity and is considered a living expense, you need to be mindful of how much you spend on it.

After you've highlighted and labeled every expense possible, take a look at the colors and dollar amounts in front of you. Do you have a large amount of bills? Are you surprised by the amount of money you've been spending on fun expenses? You will evaluate these expenses more later.

Step 2: Find the Total

To determine how much your monthly expenses are, add each category's monthly expenses together to get a total. Even if these expenses can be reduced, you won't be doing that just yet. Remember that in this step, you want to evaluate how you are *currently* managing your finances, not how you *should* manage them.

You may have some expenses that vary from month to month, like $400 for groceries in August, but only $325 in September and $350 in October. For expenses like this, you will need to determine an average, like $375. Remember that it's better to *overestimate* monthly expenses than to *underestimate* them. Once you create an actual budget, you can always come back and adjust the amounts as they change. When you have an estimated total for each category, add them together to get a grand total. This total is the amount that has been going towards expenses each month.

Step 3: Determine Your Income

To determine your income, you want to add up your monthly take home pay from any jobs you receive a paycheck for. Remember, take home pay is the amount you take home *after taxes*. If your income varies from paycheck to paycheck based on commission or hours worked, try to get a realistic average. It's better to *underestimate* your income, so only include income you make on a *regular* basis. If you helped a neighbor with a one-time home improvement project last month, that should not be included as regular income. If you do odd jobs for your neighbor every week and make a guaranteed $200-$300 a month, you can consider $200 your monthly income from that job. **Again, the golden rule is to *overestimate* your expenses and *underestimate* your income.** Add up all sources of monthly income and write down the total.

Step 4: Find the Difference

To get the difference, subtract your expenses from your income. Your number will either be positive, negative, or zero. If it's a positive number, then as it stands right now, you make more than you spend. Don't congratulate yourself just yet because you still need to factor in your debt and establish a plan to aggressively pay it down. If it's a negative number, then as it stands right now, you spend more than you make, and this book will greatly benefit you.

Step 4: Trim Your Expenses

Look at the expenses that make up each category and evaluate them one by one. Gather your utility bills for the past few months and see if there's a way you can save money by changing to a different plan or using less of that service. Be mindful of how you use your electricity and consider adjusting your thermostat to cut heating and cooling costs. Mortgage payments are normally set amounts unless you refinance, but if you currently lease, you can see if your landlord will work with you to reduce your monthly rent. Evaluate your grocery receipts to see if you could reduce costs by planning meals and only buying what you need. Look at each receipt and circle impulse buys so you can see how much they've been costing you. Expenses in the fun category can always be reduced. You don't have to deprive yourself of enjoyment, but you should limit how often and how much you spend to have fun.

Evaluate each expense and determine if it's necessary or if it can be reduced or eliminated. Instead of going out to dinner 6 times a month, perhaps you could reduce that to just once a week. Make a list of the ways you can reduce your expenses and work on them for a few weeks. In the next chapter, you will be assigning new dollar amounts to these categories and I'll discuss ways to reduce future expenses.

Chapter 2: Creating A Budget

In this chapter, you will determine where your money goes from this point forward, down to the last dollar. Being on a budget does not mean you lack money; it means you have control of your money. Even the wealthiest of people have a budget to track where their money goes. A budget is a healthy way of controlling and tracking your finances.

In order to create a budget, you need to know what expenses to include. There are several steps in this chapter, so make sure you have a fair amount of time and focus for it. You may also need to come back to this chapter several times in the first few months as you will likely have adjustments to make to your budget.

It's important to understand that when you first create a budget, it may seem like you have too many categories and not enough money, but don't let that discourage you. The whole point of this book is for you to determine how to manage your money, regardless of how much you make and how many bills you have.

Step 1: Create Categories

Grab a piece of paper and make a list of categories to include in your budget. You will want to include the specific expenses in the categories from the last chapter such as:

Mortgage/Rent	Pet Food
Car Insurance	Netflix
Car Payment	Vet Bills
Electric	Medical Costs
Cable	Gas or Bus Fare
Cell Phone	Miscellaneous
Water	Credit Card Payments
Sewer	Clothing
Trash	Restaurant
HOA Fees	Vehicle Maintenance
Monthly Parking Fees	Gift
Groceries	Home

Make sure you create a category for all of your expenses, even if they don't occur on a monthly basis. Earlier I mentioned how to break quarterly expenses down to determine monthly amounts. Some examples of these expenses include:

Vehicle Maintenance - You may need your car inspected once a year, an oil change every few months, and occasional repairs in between, so you want to set enough money aside each month to cover these costs. This eliminates the need to use a credit card or tap into your emergency savings, which I'll discuss in chapter 4. To determine a monthly dollar amount, take the cost of an oil change for example, and multiply it by the number of times you get it done over the course of a year. You then divide that number by 12 and that's your monthly amount for that expense. Think of how much you generally spend on inspections and divide that number by 12. Do this for the remaining expenses in this category and then add these amounts together to find how much you should contribute in total each month to this category.

Veterinary Bills – Pets can get sick and need regular checkups just like people. Many people stress over veterinary expenses, but if you set money aside each paycheck like I do, the only stress you'll feel about the situation is concern for your pet. Once again you will want to add up the yearly estimated costs for exams, shots, and a possible emergency visit and divide that number by 12 to find a monthly contribution amount.

Clothing - Clothing may seem like a fun category, but it's also a necessary one. You should put some money aside from each paycheck to allow yourself to shop for the things you need.

Children - If you have children, you can create categories for expenses like tuition, toys, childcare, diapers, and swim lessons.

Gift - If you make regular donations to a charity or church, you can include a gift category in your budget. I also use this category to save money for gifts around the holidays. It's surprising how much money you have at the end of the year if you put just $10 from each paycheck towards a gift category.

Home - Whether you own a home or rent an apartment, you will likely have home related expenses each year like kitchen supplies, air filters, and bedding. This category is also great for home repairs so make sure you include it in your budget!

Miscellaneous - This category is for anything that you may not account for elsewhere. I contribute $20 every paycheck to a miscellaneous category, and if I don't touch it after a few weeks I can use the money somewhere else.

These are just a few examples of categories, so please don't feel limited to only what's listed above. Every person is different and your categories will vary based on your life and your needs. Don't be shocked if after a few months, you need to add a new category. The first year of your budget can be full of changes so don't get too set in your ways. If an expense comes up that you don't have a category for, you can tap into your emergency savings and later create a category so you have money for it in the future.

When I made my first budget, I didn't include any computer related expenses even though blogging is an important form of income for me. So naturally, when my laptop died and I had to rush to the store to get it repaired, I was devastated to have to take $200 out of my emergency savings. After that, I began putting $20 a month towards a computer fund and now, if something goes wrong, I can get it repaired with the money I've set aside.

Step 2: Assign a Dollar Amount

It's easy to assign a dollar amount for some categories because the cost is the same every month, but for other categories you'll need to estimate the costs based on a few months of bills or receipts. This is where you want to *overestimate*, so if your monthly electric bill varies over a 12-month period, just focus on what the amount may be for the next 2 or 3 months. This is why you need to adjust your budget on a regular basis. You may use less air conditioning in the spring, so your bill could be around $100, but when summer hits you'll want to increase the amount you budget for this bill. If you split certain expenses with a roommate or spouse, simply divide the amount by 2.

For categories that really fluctuate, such as clothing, you want to examine your receipts and bank statements from the past 12 months and see how much you've spent. For example, if you spend around $300 every year on clothing, you can set aside $20 each month for a clothing fund. Every few months you can reward yourself with a shopping trip and stick to a budget of *only* what you have set aside for that category. Later in this book I will explain how you can plan your shopping habits around your budget so that you spend every dollar responsibly. If you know the amount you spend on clothing is unacceptably high, then you need to reduce it to a more reasonable number.

For medical expenses, it's a good idea to put money aside for copays and prescriptions, even if you don't have those expenses every month. It's like a mini savings fund for when you do need them.

Your expense amounts aren't set in stone yet because you still need to balance your budget. After doing this, you may find that certain categories are reduced or even eliminated completely.

Step 3: Create Your Spreadsheet

Now it's time to take the dollar amounts you've assigned to each category and plug them into your budget spreadsheet. You can make a spreadsheet of your own following the example in the Appendices, or you can look for one online. I offer a budget spreadsheet template for purchase on my blog at www.AskAwayBlog.com where you can plug your amounts in and the formulas are already there. If you want to use a piece of paper and a pencil, go right ahead. Stick with whatever method works best for you. If you are using the budget spreadsheet I created, there's really not much work to do aside from plugging in dollar amounts. If you run out of space for all of your categories, you can either insert new rows using the instructions in the spreadsheet or you can combine categories.

After you enter your category names and expense amounts into your spreadsheet, you can find the total and subtract that amount from your total income. If you are using my spreadsheet you can simply look at the number displayed in the 'difference' column and it will show you what you're left with after all of your expenses are subtracted from your income.

Don't let this number scare you. Remember, this is a rough draft and you can still make adjustments. Right now you will either break even, have money left over, or have expenses that outweigh your income.

Step 4: Balance Your Budget

This is the part where you adjust everything you can in order to make your budget more balanced. The changes you make to your budget don't have to be forever. My budget allowed for very few fun expenses while I was focusing on paying down my credit card debt, but once I became debt free I was able to allow myself more money for fun. The key here is to make your 'difference' a positive number. If you have a negative number, it's going to be difficult to pay down debt without anything extra to put towards it. If you break even, you still want to make some changes so that you have money left over for paying off debt and building your savings fund.

Go through your budget line by line and determine whether or not each expense is as realistically low as possible. Do you really need a latte every day or can you settle for making your own coffee at home? Is it truly necessary to dine out twice a week or can you settle for twice a month? Can you stick to buying only what's on your grocery list?

You don't have to reduce these amounts just yet because you want to make sure you can make these changes first. If you spend a few weeks being a more mindful grocery shopper, you may find that you can cut your grocery budget by $200 each month!

This is when most people have to take a few days to seriously think about where their money is going and make the commitment to change their spending and shopping habits. Remember that the whole idea of a budget is to help you see where your money currently goes and adjust where it will go in the future. As you make changes to your spending and shopping habits and reduce the amounts you put towards each expense, you may notice the 'difference' line on your budget spreadsheet getting larger. This means that you have extra money to put towards debt or add to your savings fund. Your goal is to make the 'difference' increase as much as possible.

CUTTING EXPENSES

It's important to do whatever it takes to balance your budget, even if it means temporarily eliminating some fun expenses. If you change your lifestyle *now* and spend money only when you *need* to, then *later* you can spend money where you *want* to.

It may not sound glamorous but I promise that it's worth it in the end. When I was trying to cut expenses to get myself out of debt, I changed my lifestyle to a much less glamorous one. Now that I'm debt free and manage my money well, I'm able to enjoy life with less stress and more money. I'll get into more of those details later when I tell you my story.

There are many ways to reduce your expenses but it varies based on your lifestyle. If you can drive less and save gas by carpooling to work or doing errands all at once, by all means go that route. If you can forgo your weekly movie theatre habit by signing up for a movie streaming service, go for it. Instead of monthly manicures, do your nails at home and only go to a salon every other month. You can buy clothing at consignment shops or thrift stores instead of shopping at fancy boutiques. Make a list of projects to complete in your home, like organizing every room. Instead of going out to spend money and shop, find ways to stay home and be productive. The goal is to swap big expenses for smaller ones in order to save money and still enjoy life.

Change is scary, so it's normal to feel hesitant to give up the things that make you happy. You don't need to become a hermit, but you will need to come to terms with telling your friends you can't say yes to every invitation that involves going out and spending money. While these changes may only be temporary, you might find that you like these habits and adopt them into your life forever. If the amount you contribute to certain categories seems low, keep in mind that once your debts are paid down and you establish a healthy savings fund, you can go back and increase your contribution.

Chapter 3: Creating A Cash Spending System

As much as you may be thinking about the amount of debt you have, you must first deal with your spending habits. You can't pay off your debt if you don't know how to stay out of it.

The cash spending system is where you use cash as spending money and you keep it organized in envelopes or dividers designated for each category of your budget. Many financial gurus out there swear by cash spending systems and when I started mine, I made it identical to theirs. Overtime I changed it to better suit my lifestyle, so keep in mind that my version of a cash spending system may not suit you and you are free to make changes as you see fit.

MINI SAVINGS FUNDS

Just because you have an envelope full of cash doesn't mean you should spend it right away. When I first started spending with cash, I would get overly excited at the accumulation of money and would actually look for ways to spend it. After a few months, I realized that I loved seeing a full envelope so I only spent the money if it was necessary.

The categories in your cash spending system act as mini savings funds that let you accumulate cash for when you need it most. Every few years, I would dread my car inspection because I knew that I would need new tires. Now that I use a cash spending system with a category for car expenses, I don't even flinch when it's time to pay for tires because I have a fair amount of cash set aside for that exact reason. If you have children, you may want to have a category for toys so that when Christmas or birthdays roll around, you don't have to panic about how you're going to pay for gifts.

CASH SPENDING BENEFITS

Spending with cash does something different to a person than swiping a card. When you have a card, you painlessly swipe it through a card reader and the invisible amount of money is deducted from your invisible pocket. When you spend with cash, you physically remove paper from an envelope and it suddenly becomes difficult to justify letting that $20 bill out of your hand for an impulse buy. After spending with cash for a few months, your brain adopts a new thinking process where you automatically ask yourself if you *really* need something or if you would feel better keeping the cash.

Some people insist that they *must* use their credit card because they earn rewards on everyday purchases. That isn't helping you restrict your shopping and spending, so in order to adopt better habits you need to change your behavior.

I really do believe that when I use cash, I spend it more carefully than I would with a debit or credit card. I don't like to see the cash leave my envelope, so after I have several items collected in my cart, I'll often walk through the store and put them all back. Spending with cash has forced me to re-evaluate the need for every single item I put in my cart.

YOU DON'T HAVE TO CARRY THEM

Carrying large amounts of cash can be risky, so before you write the idea off altogether, just know that you can always keep your cash somewhere safe. It's completely acceptable to leave the majority of your envelopes at home and only take them with you when you know you'll need them. Eventually you may find that you want to deposit cash from a certain category into your bank account. Just make a note that there is a specific amount in your bank account that should only be used for that category. If you're still getting used to the cash spending system then I suggest keeping your envelopes in a secure spot at home like a safe.

There's also a common misconception that people with cash spending systems walk around with thousands of dollars on them at all times. I personally never get to that point because by the time I have a large amount of money in a specific envelope; I end up having to use it. That's the whole point of the cash spending system. The categories are things that you spend money on at least once a year, so these mini savings funds are not the same as your regular savings fund or your emergency savings.

THEY DON'T HAVE TO BE ENVELOPES

Most people use envelopes for their cash spending system, but you can also use a small accordion file like the ones that people use as coupon organizers or use plastic envelopes inside a three ringed mini planner. I've even seen little fabric pouches and envelopes available online. I also know people that have so few envelopes, they choose to keep all their cash in their wallet and just separate it with little sticky notes. You can do whatever you want with this so please don't feel restricted to only the suggestions I make in this book. Feel free to get creative and allow yourself plenty of time to sit down and decide what organizational system works best for you. Don't be surprised if your cash spending system evolves over time.

My first cash spending system was a plain black coupon organizer from the dollar store, but I later transitioned to a more color fun and found the more pride I took in how I organized my cash, the more I stuck with the system. Eventually I upgraded to a Filofax personal planner, took the inserts out and replaced them with plastic zipper envelopes from an office supply store, and used a label maker to categorize them. I keep my license, debit card, and gift cards inside and use this as my everyday wallet.

No matter what method you choose, there are a few basic steps to set up your own cash spending system.

Step 1: Get Supplies

Gather your envelopes and something to label them with like a pen, marker, or label maker. You will also need a transaction log for each envelope. I have provided a sample in the Appendices that you can tear out, copy, trace, or resize. You can also make up your own tracking sheet or look around on the internet for a free printable that better suits your needs.

Step 2: Make Your Envelopes

Make an envelope, label, and log for each category you plan to use cash for. Since I pay my bills from my bank account, I don't take that money out in cash. Instead, after I take out all the cash I need for my envelopes and transfer some to my savings, my bank account is only left with the money I've budgeted for bills. You should do this for any expenses you pay electronically or with a debit card.

Step 3: Make Your Tracking Slips

I'll admit that I've been slacking on this part for the past year, but it really helps in the beginning. Each tracking slip will have the name of a category on it and as you deposit money into your envelope, you will write the date, amount, and note that it was a deposit. You will also track each time you take money from the envelope by writing the date, amount, and the reason. You may find that you begin to rethink impulse buys simply because you don't feel like logging them.

The point of these slips is to help you account for your spending and saving and to serve as a tracking system for your cash spending. Each month you should evaluate each category's expenses to see if you need to reduce the amount that you contribute.

Step 4: Fill Your Envelopes

You will be filling your envelopes every payday. My suggestion is that you have a little note in your wallet, purse, or phone that lists your categories and the amount that goes in each one every month. Some people like to physically go into the bank and take cash out in the denominations they need, but I like to use the ATM.

If you get paid bi-weekly, then on payday you divide each number by 2 and that's the amount you contribute to that envelope. Sometimes I need $10 for an envelope but the ATM only gives $20 bills, so I just take $20 out once a month. There may be some categories that only get $10 a month, which means you only need $5 from each paycheck. Since $5 is a difficult amount to get from an ATM, you can make a note to take $10 out every *other* paycheck or use smaller bills from one category to make change for big bills in another. Feel free to be creative with this part of the system and find out what works best for you. Remember that as your budget and expenses change, so will the amounts you put in each envelope.

USING A CARD INSTEAD OF CASH

Occasionally I pay for things with my debit card instead of using the cash from an envelope, so I need to readjust the amount of cash in that envelope. Say you have $20 in your fun envelope but you use your debit card to make an online fun purchase of $20. You could take that $20 from your fun envelope and on your next payday, distribute it to another category that needs $20 instead of taking $20 from the bank. You could also take the $20 from your cash envelope and deposit it into your bank account to even it all out.

Eventually you may decide to transfer $20 from a savings account to cover the cost and then on your next payday you can transfer $20 back to your savings instead of putting it in your envelope. I only suggest this method for people that consider themselves disciplined with their money because borrowing from your savings is not a good habit to get into, but occasionally it does make life easier. The cash spending system is very flexible so don't overthink it or be afraid to do something outside of what I suggested as long as it works for you and you're still being mindful with your money.

PAYING BILLS

You won't be taking out cash for expenses that you pay from your bank account like your mortgage, utilities, and credit cards. After you withdrawal the cash for your categories, your bank account will be left with only the amount of money designated for your bills. So if you get paid every 2 weeks and you pay $600 a month in rent, you should keep $300 in your checking account each payday. Make a note somewhere that tracks what each dollar left in your account is for. You can also look into opening additional shares in your bank account that you can designate for bills. On payday you would transfer a certain amount to the bill share, and when you pay that bill you transfer the amount back into your checking account.

EXTRA CASH

You may find that you have cash accumulating in certain categories that you don't end up spending by the end of the month. For most categories I recommend you keep it there, but for fun categories you can take it out and distribute it to another category that needs it more. You can also use the extra cash to pay down your debt or build your savings fund. I always keep cash in my envelopes until it gets spent so that I'm never short on cash when something unexpected comes up down the road. I look at all my envelopes as mini savings funds.

BORROWING

There's a golden rule some people follow that says you should never borrow money from another category, but sometimes it has to be done. Occasionally I buy extra groceries for a dinner I'm hosting and I spend more than I have in my grocery envelope. In that case, I will take cash from a less important category and pay it back on my next payday.

COINS

Obviously we all accumulate coins as change and they can be a bit heavy to carry around in your cash spending system, so feel free to do whatever you please with your coins. I put mine in my piggy bank and after a few months I cash them in for some extra fun money. You can use the cash you make from your coins to pay off your debt or even build up your savings fund.

Now that you have a cash spending system, make sure you use it and be mindful of how you feel when money leaves your hand. You may find yourself thinking twice before breaking a $20 bill on an impulse buy. After several months of using a cash spending system, you may notice that you spend less in certain categories, so you can adjust your budget spreadsheet accordingly. It took me 6 months of changing envelope amounts until I figured out a more realistic system for myself, so be patient.

Chapter 4: EMERGENCY SAVINGS

I capitalized this chapter because it's an important part of fixing your finances. An emergency savings is just that – a savings fund that can be used for emergencies. Before you start thinking about your debt and how to pay it down, you need to make sure you have a lump of money to use in urgent times when you would normally reach for a credit card.

I recommend starting with at least $500 in your emergency savings. As I had extra money, I would contribute more to mine until it reached $1,000. This savings is different than your regular savings because it's *only* to be used in emergencies. The great thing about the mini savings funds in your cash spending system is that they can help you with certain situations so you don't have to tap into your emergency savings.

Your emergency savings should *only* be used for *real* emergencies. A new pair of shoes that just went on sale does not qualify as a real emergency. Real emergencies are things that *have* to be dealt with and paid for *immediately* like family emergencies and urgent home repairs.

Even if you live paycheck to paycheck, you can still come up with money for your emergency savings. This should be done quickly because the sooner it's complete; the sooner you can focus on paying down your debt. Getting money together for your emergency savings might require you to step out of your comfort zone. Some people take on a second job or do odd jobs for friends and neighbors just to get the money for it. I sold some of my things online in order to fund mine. I was so eager to work on paying down my debt, that I realized I didn't need all of the unworn shoes and handbags in my closet.

A lot of people think it's impossible to come up with the money for an emergency savings, but that's why it's extremely important to do things you normally wouldn't do in order to establish one. Whether it means selling stuff online, going to a consignment shop, having a yard sale, or picking up extra hours at work, do not start paying down your debts, aside from the minimum payments, until you have established an emergency savings.

USING YOUR EMERGENCY SAVINGS

One day you may wake up to discover that your car won't start and it turns out to be a $400 fix. Since you only have $50 in your car fund, you can tap into your emergency savings and then focus on rebuilding it. You can once again sell things, pick up odd jobs, or just throw the extra money you pay towards your debt into your emergency savings. Once it's built back up, you can continue the process of paying down your debt.

You may think that you absolutely *have* to use credit cards when there's an emergency, but if you have an emergency savings you can use *that* money and you won't have to pay interest. Having an emergency savings is a crucial part of fixing your finances.

Chapter 5: Paying Off Your Debt

Being in debt is one of the worst feelings ever because it holds you back, stresses you out, and sucks up your money. While you can get things with the money you borrowed, it doesn't feel as rewarding as if you had the money to buy it with in the first place. With the exception of mortgages, car payments, and student loans, most debt is caused by things you could have paid for up front if you had managed your money well from the start.

Debt can be anything from a credit card to a student loan. Debt can even be the $500 you owe your parents for when they helped you pay for the broken pipe in your yard. At the end of the day, debt sucks! When you have debt you feel like you're never in control because it feels like you're constantly tied to someone or something since you owe *them* money.

Debt can include:
- A Mortgage
- A Car Payment
- Medical Bills
- Student Loans
- A Car Loan
- A Personal Loan
- Credit Cards

The first types of debt to get rid of are any personal loans you have. Personal loans are a priority because if you don't pay them back it can cause tension between you and the person you borrowed money from. As a rule of thumb, I advise you to never borrow money from someone unless it's a last resort. If the person you owe tells you not to worry about paying them back, consider yourself lucky. In most cases you have to pay personal loans back as soon as possible.

Next, you should tackle any medical bills you have. When you have medical bills, the billing company will constantly remind you that they *need* your money. Even if you can only pay them $50 a month, it's better than nothing at all.

Of course the most common type of debt is credit card debt. Since credit card debt is usually less than student loan debt, it's important to pay off your credit cards first. I, like many others, have had my fair share of credit card debt so that's the type of debt I'm going to focus on in this chapter. The methods used to pay down credit card debt can be applied to all forms of debt.

Paying off any kind of debt is important because you can't contribute to a savings account if all of your extra money is going to your debt. You can pay off your debts in any order you wish, but the order I'm following in this book is:
- Personal Loans
- Medical Bills
- Car Loan
- Credit Card Debt
- Student Loans
- Mortgage

Step 1: Make A List

Grab a piece of paper and write down every individual debt you have and the amount you owe on each one. This might overwhelm you as you see the dollar amounts adding up, but remember that this is a necessary and crucial step to paying down your debt.

Step 2: Create a Spreadsheet

I offer a debt pay down spreadsheet for purchase on my blog at www.AskAwayBlog.com that lets you insert your debts and the amounts you owe. You use the spreadsheet to track your payments each month and it even calculates your remaining balance for each debt. You can also use the spreadsheet example in the Appendices to create your own. Some people like using electronic spreadsheets to track things while others prefer to keep everything on paper. My spreadsheet will not calculate interest into each balance but even when I was paying down my own credit card debt, I didn't pay much attention to the interest. As long as I was paying my debt down, it was okay if the amount reflected on my spreadsheet wasn't completely accurate.

If you purchase and use the spreadsheet from my blog, all you have to do is enter in your debts and the total due for each. So if you have 3 credit cards with balances on them, they would be listed in the first column with each one getting its own cell. In the second column you enter your current balance and in the third column you enter the amount you are paying on each debt this month. In the fourth column you enter a formula (subtract the payment from the current balance) to find your new balance. In the next column you'll enter the amount you pay next month, and in the column next to that you'll again use a formula to subtract your next payment from your most current balance.

Step 3: Determine the Order

I suggest paying the minimum on each debt except the smallest one. Some people start with the debt that has the highest interest rate, but I found that when I paid the smallest debts off first, I celebrated each victory and became even more motivated for the next one.

Step 4: Determine the Amounts

In your spreadsheet you will list the minimum payment for each debt. This is the amount you're going to pay on each one, with the exception of the smallest debt. For the smallest debt you will pay the minimum payment plus anything extra you can come up with each month.

Step 5: Start Paying

Hopefully the 'difference' from your budget spreadsheet is a positive number because even if it's just $5 that you have left over each month, you can put that extra money towards your smallest debt. Pay the minimum amount on each debt every month and track it on your spreadsheet. Any extra money you have after your monthly expenses are paid can be put towards your smallest debt and tracked on your spreadsheet.

This is the part of the debt pay down process that requires some serious effort and possibly some lifestyle changes. It could take you 10 years to pay off your debt at the rate you're going now, but if you make some significant changes, it could take you just 5. You might have to drastically reduce your spending or work a second job in order to pay down your debt more quickly. Either way, you need to aggressively attack your debt like it's your sole purpose in life. Look for extra money wherever possible and consider doing an enormous clean out of your home so you can sell some of your valuables and use the profit to pay down your debt.

This is also where you will need to spend ever so carefully. If you want every extra dollar you have to go towards your debt, you have to be mindful of every extra dollar you spend. Just like when you assigned amounts to your budget categories, see if you can get those amounts even lower so that you have more money left over to put towards your debt. When you think about spending money on something, ask yourself if you would rather put it towards your debt to pay it off sooner.

Don't worry about putting money into a general savings fund right now because you have an emergency savings and some mini savings funds in your cash spending system.

Step 6: Keep Paying

As soon as you pay off your smallest debt, take the minimum amount you paid on that debt and put it towards your next debt. If your minimum payment on your smallest debt was $20 and the minimum on your next debt is $40, you want to pay $60 minimum every month in addition to throwing every extra dollar towards that next debt.

The more debts you pay off, the better it will feel and you will gain momentum and motivation along the way. Celebrate your victories and spread the great news to those around you so they can encourage you to keep going. Even if your smallest debt was $200 and you paid it off – that's a BIG deal. Some people have a chart or board where they fill in the amount of debt they've paid off along the way. Your goal is to make the process of becoming debt free fun and rewarding.

DEBT FREE

Once you've paid off your credit card debt, congratulate yourself because you are now credit card debt free! When your credit cards are paid off you can start working on your car payment if you have one, and if your student loan debt is something you can pay off in a few years, tackle that next. Some people have a massive amount of student loan debt or a mortgage that could take many years to pay off, so in that case I recommend taking a time out to build up your savings and then go back to tackling your debt.

Be realistic when it comes to debt. While I consider myself debt free because I paid off my car, my credit cards, and have no student loans, I still have a mortgage. I'm currently working on building up my savings fund a bit more before paying my mortgage off early. I know that some financial experts want you to pay off all your debt first, but I have to be realistic. I don't consider my mortgage a real debt because I know I will live in my current home for the rest of my life. I'm not worried about paying it off in a rush when there are other things I need to do with my money. Your lifestyle may be different and you may want to pay off your student loans and your mortgage right away. Just do what works best for you.

I hope this chapter has given you the basics of the debt pay down process. Remember that this is not a *must follow* guide to money. This book is a suggestive guide to help you get everything in order in the way that best suits your lifestyle.

Chapter 6 – Building A Savings Fund

You may feel like your debt will take forever to pay off, but once you've paid off your credit cards, medical bills, and personal loans, you can work on building a savings fund. Some people build up their savings fund and then go back to throwing money at larger debts like their student loans and mortgage. Having a few months' worth of expenses in your savings can ensure that you are covered in the case of an emergency and you can avoid using credit cards to get in even more debt.

IMPORTANCE OF A SAVINGS FUND

Again, the whole point of a savings fund is to save you from unexpected situations in life. You could lose your job or have to take off for a month without pay, but if you have a savings fund then you are planning for these types of scenarios. A savings fund should be able to get you through a few months of your life in the event that you don't have a way to make an income. It can also be used to cover large expenses you aren't prepared for like buying a new car because yours was totaled in an accident. Your savings fund is meant to *temporarily* get you through tough times until you have a *permanent* solution. If you have to tap into your savings fund, be sure to replace the money so that you're fully prepared for the next time you need it.

HOW MUCH TO SAVE

At minimum, I recommend having 6 months' worth of living expenses in your savings fund. Go back to your budget spreadsheet and add up your necessary living expenses like your rent, mortgage, utility bills, grocery fund, and anything else that you need in order to survive. Take that amount and multiply it by 6. This is the amount you should put in your savings fund. Your savings fund should still be separate from your emergency savings. You don't have to have a separate account, but you should not include the emergency savings money in your total savings fund amount.

HOW TO SAVE

Assuming you have already paid down your debt or that you're taking a break to build up your savings fund, you can now add an official savings category to your budget spreadsheet and begin contributing some of what you used to pay towards debt to this fund. You can also put any extra money you get from working overtime, gifts, or tax returns into your savings. Pay into your savings fund aggressively as if time is of the essence so that you can get back to paying off debts like your mortgage or student loans.

Chapter 7: Living Within Your Means

When it comes to getting your finances in order, you may have to adjust your lifestyle to really benefit financially. Some people can't understand why they live paycheck to paycheck even though their income is greater than their expenses. These people generally don't have healthy spending habits or an actual budget, so while they think they're only spending money on important things, they aren't accounting for their impulse buys.

There are 3 methods to help you live within your means, so I broke this chapter into 3 parts – spending, shopping, and saving. Spending habits pertain to the way you decide to spend your money, shopping habits pertain to the way you actually spend your money, and saving habits deal with your ability to save money rather than spend it.

SPENDING HABITS

Healthy spending habits take some practice, but it becomes easier the more you work on it. The healthy way to spend money is to find enjoyment in affordable ways. Let me give you an example.

Say you enjoy watching movies and you have a habit of buying a new DVD every week. Do you really need all of those DVDs? Do you watch them more than once a year? If you purchase one DVD a week at $20 each, that amounts to $80 a month. Most people assume that the way to fix this habit is to just stop buying DVDs altogether, but that won't bring you any joy and you likely won't stick to it. Instead of stripping yourself of the joy you get from watching movies, choose a more affordable way to watch them by signing up for a DVD rental or streaming service. The monthly cost will surely be less than a weekly DVD purchase.

Say you love getting your nails done once a month at the salon as a way to pamper yourself. That money adds up quickly, so perhaps you can go to the store and find a nice manicure set with similar tools to the ones they use in the salon. You can take time each week to do your own nails and only visit the salon every other month. Again, you don't have to give it up altogether; just change how often you go.

When you restrict your spending, it can help you think of alternatives at a lower cost that still benefit you. This is why the cash spending system is a great way to practice holding onto cash and thinking before you spend it. You don't have to deprive yourself of the things you enjoy because the whole point of a fun category is so you have money to spend on fun.

Think of everything you purchase as an investment. Is it just going to take up space in your home and make it feel cluttered or is it going to be something you love every single day? Ask yourself questions like this each time you go to spend money, whether it's $5 or $50.

SHOPPING HABITS

I used to love shopping just because I liked the feeling of carrying multiple bags out of a store. I would go to a department store and buy several shirts. These shirts wouldn't have the perfect fit, but I thought they looked cute on display so I bought them anyways. The majority of them would sit in my closet for over a year with the tags still on and I eventually purged them. What a waste of money!

I also used to walk through stores and gather little knick-knacks on my way to the register. I still do that from time to time, but now as I walk through the store, I ask myself questions about the items in my cart. It's to the point now where I don't even put them in my cart. Instead, I hold them and ask myself if it's really worth the money and most of the time it's not so I put them back.

Impulse buys can really suck money out of your budget. Whether it's a shirt or a candy bar, you *can* control your impulses with enough discipline and practice. Obviously if you don't have the money in your cash spending system, you should put the item back. If you do have the money, you need to ask yourself if it's really worth breaking a $20 bill or is there something else you would rather spend your money on. Impulse buys can happen anywhere, even at the grocery store.

GROCERIES

Speaking of grocery shopping – while it's necessary to buy groceries, you can still be mindful of the amount you spend and what items you're buying. There are plenty of stores that offer reduced price groceries where people can save hundreds of dollars each month. Even if you stick with your usual grocery store, you can choose to buy generic brands. Coupons are great, but only use them if you need the specific brand and item advertised. Often times, generic brands can still cost less than the regular brand, even with a coupon discount. The number one thing I do to save money on groceries is to only buy what I need and to choose generic 95% of the time. I'm also a huge advocate of meal planning.

MEAL PLANNING

Meal planning is a great way to save money and stay organized with your schedule. Some people rush around in the evenings only to realize they didn't eat dinner, have nothing in the fridge, and end up ordering pizza. Meal planning can help you prepare healthier meals and eliminate the need for impulse buys. Look around on the internet and find at least 20 recipes or meal ideas that suit you and your family's needs. I offer some free printable recipes on my blog at www.AskAwayBlog.com. Next, make a weekly calendar or search around for a free meal planning printables. Each week you will go through your recipes, choose next week's meals, and fill out your calendar. Then you will make your grocery list based on the ingredients you need for each recipe. As you make your list, make sure you check stock in your pantry so you aren't buying duplicates and letting things in your cupboard go to waste. You can also add the regular items you're low on such as drinks, lunch items, breakfast, and toiletries. The key is to go through your life on a daily basis in your head, think of everything you use and eat, and base your list off of what you need.

If you go to the grocery store without a list, you're just asking to spend more than you should. When you shop at the grocery store, *only* buy what's on your list. If you get tempted and buy other things, then you are spending more than you need to. Set your list up in the order of where the aisles are so you can zip through the store and avoid distractions.

Meal planning can help you eat fresh foods and make healthier choices. I used to buy frozen meals every week and had an excess supply in my freezer. Not only was I missing out on eating healthy meals, but I would end up throwing away meals that expired and it was a total waste of money.

SAVING HABITS

Once you've balanced your budget, paid down a fair amount of debt, and built up an emergency savings, you should still plan on putting money aside each month. After you become debt free, you will likely have some extra money to add to your regular savings fund. It may be tempting to go on a spending spree to celebrate your debt-free life, but you need to stay in a healthy mindset. Save all the money you can and after you have a decent savings fund built up, continue to put money aside while giving yourself some extra spending cash.

When you get money as a gift, put it directly into your savings. Remember that a savings account is crucial to your life because it can help you get through worst case scenarios.

Chapter 8: Credit Cards

Credit cards can be a touchy subject and my opinion on them may not be the same as everyone else's, but sometimes you have to do what works best for you.

PAYING THEM OFF

While you are in the process of paying off credit card debt, you should cut up your cards or lock them away so you don't have them available for an impulse buy. I cut up all my cards except one, which I kept in case of a huge emergency since my savings account wasn't fully funded.

Even if you get credit card rewards, you should stop using credit cards while you're paying them off. In order to teach yourself how to only spend with money you currently have, you need to avoid borrowing money. Most people aren't disciplined enough at this point, which is why they are in so much debt to begin with, so using a credit card is flirting with danger.

CREDIT SCORES

I'm not an expert on credit scores, but I do know from experience that as long as you have a balance on your cards and you make your minimum payments on time, you *will have* one. There are several ways that you can maintain a decent credit score.

First, keep your balances low. If your total available line of credit is $10,000 and you only carry a balance of $3,000, you will have a better credit to debt ratio than someone who carries a balance of $8,000. The bigger the gap, the more it can help your credit score.

Even when I carried an enormous balance on my credit cards, my score was in the high 700's as I paid them down because I kept them open. If you pay off a card, you shouldn't rush to close it. You can cut it up or lock it away, but since your credit to debt ratio affects your credit score it looks better to have a large available balance.

It's also important to be aware of your credit score. You can get a free credit report once a year from AnnualCreditReport.com. Every year, this website will give you a separate report from each of the nationwide credit reporting companies – Equifax, TransUnion, and Experian. It's important that you monitor and review your credit report. When you apply for a loan or look for credit, lenders pull your report which can put a slight dent in your credit score. When you get your annual credit report make sure you read it carefully and if you see anything odd make sure you look into it.

It's also important to pay your bills on time. This goes a long way if you ever have to deal with a credit card company to get a lower interest rate because you can remind them that you're reliable and have never missed a payment.

STRUGGLING TO PAY YOUR DEBTS

If you're struggling to pay down a debt like a medical bill, it's important to pay a small amount rather than nothing at all. If you have a company hounding you for payments, you can tell them that you can only afford to pay a certain amount per month and they will most likely be willing to work with you until you're able to give them more.

If you're looking at your list of debts and you feel stressed because there's no possible way you can pay the required minimum on every single debt each month, pick up the phone and be prepared to bargain with the lender.

CASH TALKS

Some people are completely set on the idea that you can't get financing if you don't have an amazing credit score, but cold hard cash has a voice that speaks to almost anyone. I know of people that had poor credit when trying to lease an apartment, so they offered to pay the first 2 months' rent up front in cash to their landlord. In most cases, their landlord gladly took the cash and waived the credit score requirement. Having money up front can show that you are somewhat responsible with your finances. Sometimes a credit score suffers because a person doesn't carry a balance on their credit cards and hasn't used them in years. A credit score doesn't define you so always be willing to prove your capabilities in another way.

Ellen Ross

CREDIT CARD REWARDS

Credit cards that offer cash back rewards can be very beneficial when used correctly. If you haven't paid off your credit card debt, then you shouldn't use a credit card at all. I'll explain this part by telling you my own experience with credit card rewards.

About a year after I became debt free, I decided to apply for a cash back rewards credit card. I did my research and applied for one with no annual fees, 1% cash back on all purchases, and 3% cash back on qualifying purchases each quarter like groceries and fuel. Since the qualifying purchases are things I spend money on every month anyways, I knew this card would benefit me more than a card offering rewards for travel.

When payday comes around, I take the cash I'd normally take out for groceries and I transfer it to a share in my bank account that I call the grocery fund. When I go grocery shopping, I use my cash back rewards credit card and then as soon as I get home, I take out my receipt and transfer the amount I spent at the store from my grocery fund to my checking account. Then, I log into the credit card account and make a payment for the amount I just spent on that card. This way I never get charged interest because I pay everything off right away but I still get cash back rewards. At the end of the year, I can use my cash back rewards for Christmas gifts or to put towards a large purchase for myself.

REWARDS FOR OPENING A CREDIT CARD

Have you ever been shopping and when you get to the cash register the cashier asks you if you would like to open a store card today? When you say no she quickly reminds you that you're missing out on getting 30% off today's purchase and she even lets you know what your new total would be after the discount. You could certainly say yes and open an account, which will put a small dent in your credit score since they pull your report, and then pay off the card when you get home and never use it again. This might work perfectly for you *if* you're disciplined with your spending and you don't mind the extra work. If you're *not* disciplined, this could be dangerous since you know you have a credit card for that store and it may influence you to shop there more often. This is when some people start using a credit card without paying it off right away. Sometimes they even pay it off with money that was designated to go towards something else and it offsets their budget.

So this is where you have to ask yourself if the temporary 30% off is worth the risk. Maybe it isn't and you'll politely decline or maybe it is and you'll accept, get the discount, and cancel the card as soon as you get home.

I end up saying no to all credit card offers when I'm shopping because at the end of the day my cash spending system works best for me. After I have a decent amount of money saved up in my clothing envelope, I'm very careful with how I spend it because I want to get the most out of every dollar. Instead of splurging on one pair of shoes, I'll shop around to find the best deal on an affordable pair and still have money left over for something else. Credit cards don't always allow you to practice healthy spending and saving habits, which is why I recommend you decline any offers you receive from the cashier.

SPECIAL FINANCING

Sometimes the need to make a large purchase is inevitable. Refrigerators can suddenly stop working, laptops can burn out, cars can break down, and that's when we panic because we don't have an extra $2,000 to cover the cost. Even if you have a savings fund, it may not have enough to cover the full cost. So what does one do in this situation? Once again I'll explain my personal experience with financing.

As a blogger, my laptop is my lifeline. I purchased my first laptop in my early 20's when I was young and irresponsible. I carried my laptop everywhere, spilled crumbs and liquids on it, and dropped it more than a handful of times. After a few years, I noticed that my laptop would overheat more frequently while I was editing photos or watching videos. In order to save itself from any major damage, it would automatically shut down, causing me to lose my work. I knew the end was near and I had already spent money getting it repaired several times before, so I did some research on the problem. It seemed my laptop's body style wasn't designed for proper ventilation and this was a common issue. The new body style was designed to prevent overheating, so I knew this would be a worthy investment to help my blogging income.

I checked the brand's website for special financing deals and sure enough, there was a credit card with 0% interest for the first 18 months as well as a nice discount on your first purchase. Since I was credit card debt free and comfortable with managing my money, I knew I could pay the card off in less than 18 months with the extra money in my budget. I paid the card off within 6 months and cut it into tiny pieces. This is a situation where it pays to use special financing. If the credit card was not interest free for 18 months, I likely would not have made the purchase and would have saved more money in my computer fund first.

I take good care of my new laptop and back it up every week so that if it crashes I won't lose all my work. I don't eat or drink near my laptop and I keep it one or two locations rather than carrying it all over the place and running the risk of dropping it.

BUYING A VEHICLE

Most of us need a vehicle to run errands, travel, and commute to work. Before you start shopping for a new car, you should look at your budget and see how much money you can put towards a car payment. You may think that buying a vehicle is pretty cut and dry, but there are some important things to think about first.

Think long-term. Forget everything you hear about what car is the fastest and which one is the most stylish. It's time to be realistic and think in the long-term. You want a reliable car that will last a long time and require affordable routine maintenance. I had several used cars as a teenager that would cost so much to pass inspection each year that I had to use my credit card and I ended up accumulating a significant amount of debt. When my clunker of a car finally blew its transmission, it was time for me to make a smart purchase. For years I heard people talk about how fuel efficient and reliable their Hondas were. That type of car always stuck out in my mind, so when it came time to shop for a new car, I went straight to the local Honda dealership. I felt it would be the best purchase for me since it would last a long time, get great gas mileage, and require affordable maintenance.

Should you lease or buy? I'm not really going to talk about leasing because I don't fully understand it. It's never been the right decision for me because when I purchase something, I plan to keep it until it falls apart. Some people enjoy changing vehicles every few years so leasing is a better option for them.

Basically, when you lease a car you are paying someone else to let you borrow it for a set amount of time. Dealerships often advertise low monthly payments for leasing a vehicle, but it's important to read the fine print. There are usually other terms to the lease like having to pay a few thousand bucks up front to get a lower payment, as well as being restricted by the dealer in regards to how many miles you can put on the car in a certain amount of time.

When you lease a car, it's a bigger issue if someone dings your car door because in the end, you can get penalized for the damage. Leasing a car means that you don't actually own it and eventually you have to give it back. I recommend anyone interested in leasing a vehicle to do plenty of research before going down that path. Again, it's not necessarily a bad thing but it just doesn't make the most financial sense in my opinion.

If you buy a car, you can pay it off, and then it's yours! Even in the worst situation, no one can take it from you because you officially own it once it's paid off. It feels so great to not have a car payment and when you own your car you can sell it whenever you want, modify it however you wish, and put as many miles on it as you please.

New or Used? New cars are very appealing because they're shiny, attractive, and in mint condition – never owned by another soul until you came along. Unfortunately, when you purchase a new car, you lose money as soon as you drive it off the lot because it's officially a used car. Often times when people hear the term 'used' in connection with vehicles, they picture a beat up rusty old car with high mileage. In reality, many dealerships offer quality pre-owned vehicles at a great price. You can get a great deal on a used vehicle simply because someone *else* drove it off the lot and lost money on it.

When I went to the dealership to look for a new car, I was getting estimates that were well over $20,000 when all was said and done. To me, that just seemed like too much money to spend on my first car. So I went home to think about it, came back the next day with my dad, and at his suggestion started looking around the pre-owned section of the dealership's lot.

When I first saw my car, it was like a scene from a movie. I thought I saw every available car and was losing hope since nothing caught my eye. Everything seemed to have high mileage, a manual transmission, and 2 doors instead of 4. My dad and I both noticed a car pull away from the lot, revealing a very attractive gray car behind it that we didn't notice the first time. My dad walked over and read the sticker. For $16,995 this 2006 Honda Civic had only 4,848 miles, no accidents, and was a 4-door automatic. My current car only had a trade in value of $300 since the transmission was blown, but even without any extra money down, I was able to get financing from a credit union at the age of 19 for the total cost of just over $19,000. I even received a double warranty since my car was still covered under the previous owner's new car warranty. My payment was $375 a month. It wasn't easy to convince my dad that I was making the right choice, which leads me to my next point.

Think long-term, AGAIN. Before I actually purchased my car, I went home to think about it, and my dad reminded me that I still had the option of putting $1,000 into my current car and driving it for a few more years. I spent a few hours thinking about my options. I was 19 years old and had just started a full time career with the state. I still lived at home and didn't plan on moving out for a few more years. I knew that with a newer car, especially a Honda, the maintenance costs are very low for the first 10 years. Aside from new tires, brakes, and oil changes, nothing should go wrong as long as I maintain it meticulously. If I kept my current car, I'd continue to pay several thousand dollars a year on maintenance for a car that I wasn't sure would last much longer. In several years I would be paying rent for an apartment and trying to save for a house, so I wouldn't have the money to buy a car if mine suddenly decided to break down again for good. I knew that if I bought a newer vehicle *now*, I would be 30 and in much better financial shape by the time it turns 10 and needs more maintenance. I also needed a reliable car to get me to and from work since I had started my career and couldn't afford to miss work due to breakdowns and overheating. I assured my dad that in 10 years I would be even happier with my decision, and went back to the dealership the next day to sign the papers.

It's been over 10 years since I first got my Honda and she now has just over 100,000 miles. Aside from oil changes, tires, and brakes, she has not needed any major maintenance. I set $20 aside every paycheck for car expenses so that by the time inspection rolls around, I always have money for anything she needs. I plan to keep her until she turns to dust, which I'm positive will be well over 5-10 years from now.

Duration of the loan. By the time I was 22, I was in a tough financial situation where I could barely afford my rent and I had a significant amount of credit card debt that I needed to pay down if I ever wanted to buy a house. So I refinanced my loan and extended it from 5 years to 6. Some people would say that was a bad decision, but I knew without a doubt that my car would last well beyond that extra year. I also knew that this was only temporary and if I had a lower car payment, even just for a year or two, I could go back to paying it off in less than 6 years once my financial situation improved. By extending my loan to 6 years, my payment went down to $220 a month. The extra $155 I saved each month helped me immensely and I still paid my car off in just over 5 years. This might not be reasonable for everyone but it's what I had to do at the time to get by and I'm almost positive that if I didn't have that extra money each month, I would have made even more bad decisions with credit cards. Sometimes you have to explore a variety of options to figure out what works best for you.

So if you are in desperate need of a newer vehicle and can only afford a low monthly payment, consider a quality pre-owned vehicle from a reliable manufacturer. Don't be afraid to take out a longer loan as long as there's no penalty if you pay it off early. Your monthly payment will be lower and that may help you for the first few years. Although it means you'll pay more in interest if you take the full 6 years to pay it off, you may find that after 2 years, you can afford to pay more and you can pay your car off early. Just keep throwing all the extra money you have each month at your car loan. Again, some people would not suggest taking out a longer loan for a car, but I stand behind quality car manufacturers that go well beyond 10 years of ownership. As long as you buy a reliable vehicle and maintain it responsibly, you should have no regrets.

Establish a car fund. A car fund is crucial for anyone with a vehicle because every car out there needs money put into it for gas, maintenance, and cleaning. I currently put $20 from each paycheck into my car fund in my cash spending system and after a few months, I have several hundred dollars saved. A car fund helps you practice healthy saving habits and also allows you to take proper care of the car you own. If you neglect your car and never keep up with the maintenance, eventually you'll *have* to deal with it all at once and it will likely break the bank. Trust me when I say that planning ahead is critical.

Maintain your vehicle like it's brand new. You should take pride in everything you own, and your car is no exception. Vacuum and wipe down the interior every month and make sure you wash and wax the outside. If you have no clue what routine maintenance your car needs, then look online or call a dealership. There are many things that go into proper maintenance in the life of a vehicle like timing belts, spark plugs, and system flushes. If you don't take care of your car, the only person it hurts in the end is you. Neglecting your car is the same as neglecting your health. If you don't take care of your health, you can start breaking down, and a car is no different. The more you ignore crucial things like belts and oil changes, the more you risk your car breaking down and costing you more in the end. Be smart and responsible when it comes to your vehicle. You can cut costs on maintenance by learning how to do things yourself or paying an experienced friend or neighbor to do the work.

Chapter 9: Changes

It's important to understand that getting your finances in order is a never-ending process. Even when you finally get them in order you will need to maintain them, but once you complete the initial setup it's much easier to manage along the way. We're all human and our income, expenses, and the way we spend our money will change over time. The key is to continue altering your budget and spending habits so you can live within your means.

DON'T BECOME TOO SET IN YOUR WAYS

Even the most organized people need to allow for changes in their finances. While you did the initial set up and created a system that works for you, you will still have to keep your system updated. I usually adjust my budget spreadsheet every few months as my bills decrease or my income increases. The benefit of doing all the work in the first place is that it's easier to go in and make minor adjustments along the way. You might even create new categories for your cash spending system.

LIFE HAPPENS

Unfortunately, there are things in life that no one can plan for like the sudden loss of a loved one, major health issues, or a natural disaster. When something like this happens, it's completely acceptable to forget everything you've worked on for a few weeks and take care of yourself mentally, physically, and emotionally. Things will come up where you have to spend some cash on something that isn't in your budget and that's okay. Don't let this type of thing stress you out when you already have plenty to worry about. When life settles down you can get back on track.

HOLIDAYS

The holidays can be a dangerous time for anyone trying to be mindful of their spending. While we tend to get in the spirit of giving, we often neglect our own financial needs. Giving gifts can bring joy to others, but it's important to remember that not every gift has to be purchased. You can offer services like a free day of cleaning for a close friend or family member in the form of a handmade certificate. You can also spend a little money up front to get supplies and create your own homemade body scrub to gift someone. Always be practical around the holidays.

Another great idea is to start the holiday season off in an organized manner by determining every person you need to purchase a gift for and writing their names down on paper. Next to each name put a dollar amount you wish to spend. This is where you will use the money you have set aside in your gift envelope or Christmas fund, and think of gift ideas that stay under your budgeted amounts. I do this every year and still come up with great gifts. Sometimes I even use gift cards and coupons towards purchases for other people. The best type of gift is often an experience, so take someone to dinner, see a movie, attend a concert, or go on a hike together. If possible, try to work on getting out of the habit of having to buy "things" as gifts. Some people will desperately shop around just to find some random "thing" that the recipient doesn't need and will likely discard in a year or so.

Chapter 10: Lifestyle Changes

If you're in a very unhealthy financial situation, you need to consider making some major lifestyle changes. The problem most people have is that they get too stuck in their ways and refuse to step out of their comfort zone. If you go out of your comfort zone *now*, you can get in a better financial situation *later*.

ADDITIONAL EMPLOYMENT

I know you're probably cringing at the thought of having to get a second job, but if after reducing your expenses, they're still more than your income, you need to find a way to bring in more money. If you don't, your situation may never improve and will likely get worse. A second means of income doesn't have to be an actual job that you drive to every evening. It can be as simple as doing something that you're good at for a small fee. If you enjoy cleaning and organizing, offer to do it on a weekly or monthly basis for your friends, family, and neighbors. You can advertise your services on a local internet marketplace. You can also make money off of your hobbies. If one of your favorite hobbies is making jewelry, try to sell some of your greatest work. If you let your friends and family know that you are working extra hard to get more money to pay off a debt or build your savings, they may be more than willing to help you out.

HOW YOU SPEND YOUR FREE TIME

In addition to working a side job in your spare time, you may have to make some adjustments with your spending habits. This may require you to decline invitations you receive and stay home more often. You don't need to completely give up your social life, but you do need to make better decisions and balance your spending with your income.

MAKE EXTRA CASH WHENEVER YOU CAN

Yard sales and consignment shops are a great way to make extra cash from things you no longer need. An brilliant way to stay home and avoid going out and spending money is to start the great project of purging, cleaning, and organizing your entire home. You will be surprised by how many things you find that you can sell for a few extra bucks.

GETTING ORGANIZED

People often tell me that once they have their finances in order, they realize how disorganized the rest of their life is. I'm going to let you in on a little secret that will not only help your budget, but also your everyday life. Purge and organize every aspect of your life. Taking on the project of purging and reorganizing your entire home can help you in several ways. When you have an orderly home it's easy to see what you already have, so you aren't buying excess stuff and spending money when you don't need to. Don't buy something unless you absolutely love it or need it. Try to keep a clutter-free home that isn't lined wall to wall with furniture containing knick-knacks on display that just get dusty and create more cleaning for you. You may also find that your health habits need improvement, so spend time taking walks and practice meal planning so you can eat healthier foods.

GOODS vs. EXPERIENCES

Ever since I learned to manage my finances, I choose to spend my money on experiences rather than material goods. I used to spend my fun money on fast food, knick-knacks, or impulse buys, but now I put that money towards concerts, wine tastings, and dinners with friends.

When I'm shopping, I think twice before I buy something. Material goods are often purchased on an impulse and eventually we purge them from our homes. Then they either end up in a landfill or they become an unnecessary possession in someone else's home. I used to think that shopping for clothing brought me joy, when in reality it was the nice quality clothing itself that made me happy. So now I shop only when I need something and I take my time to find the best quality item. Not only do I spend my cash more wisely, but I spend my free time in more productive ways.

Chapter 11: My Story

There's a reason I'm telling you my story towards the end of this book, rather than the beginning. I didn't want to deter anyone who couldn't relate to my financial experiences. A bad financial situation can happen to anyone, anywhere, at any time, and I was no different.

I always thought I made the right decisions growing up, which I still think is true, but you can only make a decision based on what you know about the matter at hand. I, like most people, wasn't really educated on how to manage money.

After I turned 16 and passed my driver's test, I started my first real job making $8 an hour as a cashier at an office supply store. I borrowed my parents' car to get there until they bought me my first used car for around $4,000 and I started a monthly payment plan to pay them back. I made sure to work any extra hours I could at my job and when school was out for the summer, I gladly agreed to work weekday hours in addition to weekends. I truly believe that having a job as soon as I was old enough, really helped me understand that *any* type of job is necessary to earn money and afford the things I need and want in life.

I eventually took a job as a cashier at a grocery store and couldn't stand it, so I quit at the end of my senior year and spent that summer looking for a serious full time job. What's funny is that most people assumed I was being a typical teenager and taking the summer off, but that was far from the truth.

That summer, I mowed 3 lawns a week in my neighborhood for $25 each. I needed new tires on my car by the end of summer, so I made sure to put some of that money aside. Still, I didn't deprive myself of fun. I was able to stretch my mowing money throughout the summer to pay for gas in my car, monthly manicures, and dinners with my friends. By the end of the summer, I was still able to purchase 4 new tires for my car.

I spent that entire summer applying for jobs, often sending my resume to several places a day. At the end of summer, I started my first full time job as a receptionist at a staffing agency's office. My mom had worked for the state for a few years at this point and I wanted to do the same, so as soon as I turned 18 I took the civil service test and started interviewing for jobs at the state. My receptionist job didn't offer paid time off so I knew it would be difficult to take off work for an interview. This next part is why I tell everybody that everything really does happen for a reason, and sometimes it doesn't make sense until you look back on it.

One day I received word that I was being laid off through no fault of my own, and as much as it crushed me, I reminded myself that someday it would make sense. On the bright side, I could collect unemployment and interview for state jobs without worrying about my work schedule. I focused all of my energy on interviews and waiting for the right opportunity in an office I would truly enjoy. After 2 months of interviewing, I accepted an entry level clerical position and at the age of 18 I began my full time career with the state. I was ecstatic to have a real career with great pay, full benefits, and paid time off.

Unfortunately, I still didn't understand the concept of budgeting and being mindful of my spending, so I continued to use my credit cards without much thought. After my first year with the state I was able to buy my own car, as I discussed in an earlier chapter, but the rest of my money was spent frivolously.

I can't tell you how difficult the first 2 or 3 years at my job were because while I was waking up at 6 am every day; I had friends that were just living it up at home until they figured out what they wanted to do with their life. Some of them went to college, which is great, but it just wasn't for me. I didn't want the debt from student loans and I had no idea what I wanted to do with my life so I didn't want to commit to any specific major. When I told my mom how frustrated I felt about being one of the few people my age to have a serious career already, she advised me to stick with it because in a few years when others were struggling to find a job, I would already be set in mine. She was right. I started at an entry level position and have worked my way up over the past 10 years.

When I was 22, I moved into my first apartment but still had no clue how to manage my money. It's amazing that I got by as well as I did at the time; then again, living paycheck to paycheck while using a credit card for living expenses isn't really "getting by". Of course life happened, as it always does, and I went through a few bad breakups and the tragic loss of my best friend who passed away when I was 22. The combination of events left me pretty bummed out and I began suffering from anxiety and depression. By the time I began to see a therapist and start medication, the damage to my finances had already been done.

You see my method of coping with feeling sad and lonely was to get home from work and immediately head out to go shopping and make myself feel better. It actually got to the point where I couldn't even walk through a convenience store without picking up a few random items near the check out. Even my friends began to notice and make little comments about it. Shopping seemed to fill a void for me and since I lived by myself, I never had to worry about someone telling me it was absurd to come home with 5 or 6 shopping bags a night.

Due to some other unfortunate circumstances a few years later, I had to move back home with my parents. While I was, and still am grateful to have that option, at 26 years old living at home with your my parents wasn't ideal. I paid a small amount of rent each month and purchased my own groceries, toiletries, and anything else I needed. I did my own laundry and helped out around the house by sweeping, doing dishes, and organizing things. It was frustrating at times, but I kept reminding myself that it was going to be worth it someday. I now had the chance to focus on paying off my debt and saving up for a house; and that's just what I did.

I lived very frugally in my 2 years at home. I stuck to a grocery list like it was my sole mission in life. I planned out every day's breakfast, lunch, dinner, and snacks. I didn't buy any clothing except absolute necessities. I didn't take vacations or go to many events unless it was free to get in or had a low cover fee. I sold anything nice I had that I didn't mind letting go of. I also turned my focus to building up my blog to get more traffic. I knew that my blogging income could help me get out of debt faster and it was a race against time because the sooner I got out of debt, the sooner I could look for a house.

Every single extra dollar I made went towards my debt. Prior to moving home, I was trying to pay more than the minimum payment on my debts but I could never get ahead after my bills were paid, so I barely made a dent in even my smallest credit card. At the time, moving back home with my parents was the absolute best and most realistic option for me.

In the end it paid off, and I mean that quite literally. On April 17th, 2015 I became debt free. My car was already paid off and every single credit card I had a balance on was now at zero. One month later, on May 17th, 2015 my boyfriend and I stumbled upon *the* perfect house with everything we ever wanted, in the exact neighborhood we had wanted, and at a price that we could afford. It was like a dream come true and if I hadn't become debt free a month prior, I would not have even noticed this house. Like I said, everything happens for a reason. One month later, on June 17th, 2015 we settled on our first home. Isn't it crazy how much can happen in 3 months? It's like everything fell into place.

I consider our home a forever home because we have no plans to move again until we are very old and it's beyond our control. We do not plan to start a family, aside from pets, so a 3 bedroom home is perfect.

The process of purchasing a home isn't as glamorous as I made it seem. I was very stressed because we didn't have any money to put towards a down payment. Luckily we were able to get the seller to cover some of the closing costs and my boyfriend paid for the rest with the money he had set aside after becoming debt free a year prior. Our house is our only debt and we plan to refinance down the road. We also plan to pay it off early by doubling up on payments each year.

Owning a house is a wonderful thing but it also comes with many expenses. While I'm still piling money away in savings, I'm also trying to put some towards little things that are needed around the house like minor repairs and upgrades. Being a homeowner in control of my finances makes the experience that much better. I don't buy home decor unless it's beautiful or serves a purpose. I choose to invest in high quality pieces that bring me joy. I have more energy to focus on saving money for upgrades down the road, and it's nice being able to focus on just one thing at a time. It's been a few years since I began managing my money the correct way and I find that it comes so naturally now.

CHAPTER 12: How I Live Now

My fairy tale ending still needs to be maintained or it could become a nightmare. All it takes is some careless credit card spending and I could spiral out of control. Since I enjoy managing my money and find it rewarding, it's very easy for me to maintain my habits. I often remind myself of how miserable I was all those years that I was drowning in debt.

I remain disciplined with my shopping habits and I don't let discount offers get the best of me. While store credit cards may help me get a percentage off my entire order, I run the risk of using it when I don't have the money to pay it off. I refuse to let myself go down that path again so I always decline the offer.

I drive my car like it's made of gold. I take pride in my home and take good care of everything inside of it. I am mindful of how I use electricity and I meal plan every single dinner with the exception of a pizza delivery night once a month.

When I'm not at my full time job, I work on my blog and even though it takes up my time, it's rewarding because the extra income I make each month can go towards my savings.

My home is neat and organized. I can tell you where everything is and name everything I own because I only possess things that bring me joy or serve a purpose. Cleaning my house is a simple weekly task and I'm always prepared if a surprise guest stops by.

I have 4 Chihuahuas that bring an incomprehensible amount of joy to my life. I make it a priority to put money aside for veterinary costs, food, and anything else they may need. I always make sure I put enough money aside from each paycheck to cover an emergency.

I also have a very short commute to work so I don't have to worry about gas or wear and tear on my car. My home is located centrally to every store I would need to get to, and we made sure to buy a house with a garage so our cars can stay safe at night and during bad weather.

While I love clothing, I only own things that I will wear on a regular basis. I make the most out of each article of clothing in my closet and I mix and match a lot between seasonal wardrobes which helps me make the most of every dollar I spend on clothing. Even if something looks beautiful, if it doesn't feel comfortable when I wear it, I won't buy it.

I have money set aside for holidays and special occasions and I shop very carefully to ensure that I make the most of every single penny in my gift budget. I consider giving to those in need good karma, so I make a few charitable donations throughout the year.

I reuse items that I already own instead of going out to buy new ones. The file folders I use in my office drawers already had writing on them so I simply placed a new label on top.

I try to be practical with how my home is set up. For example, I got rid of the majority of DVDs I owned because I didn't watch them anymore. I now only need one shelf of my bookcase for the few DVDs I kept and I use the other shelves for my decorative items. Since I own fewer possessions, I have more time to clean and relax and I truly feel less stressed.

Fixing my finances was only the first step in a complete lifestyle change. Every decision I make is now based on a long term end result. I can't remember the last time I actually had an impulse buy in my life.

CHAPTER 13: Just the Beginning

While you may be at the end of this book, this is just the beginning for you. Take your time and use the methods in this book to gradually change your lifestyle for the better. It's completely acceptable to alter the way things are done to better suit your needs. Not everyone will have the same expenses or debts as I do.

I tried to make this book as realistic as possible. I've read about people that make drastic changes in their life like only having 1 car for the entire family or not having cable and internet, and while those are very impressive measures to take, they certainly aren't for everyone. I personally love having my own car and my cable TV shows bring me joy.

The idea of having to get a second job isn't very appealing at first, but that's why I suggest using your free time to do the things you already enjoy in a way that can benefit you financially. I enjoy writing and I wouldn't know what to do without my blog. I love what I do, regardless of how much money it makes me.

Whatever you decide to do, I truly hope this book has helped you better understand your finances so you can get on the right track for a better future. Never give up hope, because it *is* possible to fix your finances. If I can do it, so can you!

Appendices

BUDGET SPREADSHEET EXAMPLE

MONTHLY TAKE HOME	
MONTHLY SPENDING	$0.00
DIFFERENCE	$0.00
NAME OF EXPENSE	**MONTHLY COST**
MONTHLY SPENDING	$0.00
TOTAL (Spending - Income)	$0.00

CASH ENVELOPE TRACKER

Category Name:		
Date	Expense/Deposit	Amount

DEBT TRACKER

Debt	Due Date	Starting Amount	Jan 16		Feb 16	
			Pmt	Total	Pmt	Total
Card Name	25th	$10,000.00	$100.00	$9,900.00		$9,900.00
Loan Name	30th	$1,000.00	$20.00	$980.00		$980.00
				$0.00		$0.00
				$0.00		$0.00
				$0.00		$0.00
				$0.00		$0.00
Total		$11,000.00	$120.00	$10,880.00	$0.00	$10,880.00

ADDITIONAL RESOURCES

You can find more information on my blog at:
www.AskAwayBlog.com
Click on the FINANCE tab

You can email me with any questions at:
EllenR886@gmail.com

You can follow me via social media at:
Facebook:
Facebook.com/AskAwayAdviceBlog
Twitter:
@ellen_ross1
Instagram:
@ellenr886